The Hatfields and the McCoys

The Dramatic Story of a Mountain Feud

JOHN R. SPEARS

A. J. Cornell Publications

Copyright © 1888 *Current Literature* magazine

ISBN: 1484008642
ISBN-13: 978-1484008645

CHAPTER 1

The people of the North have read short sketches of incidents of the deadly feuds between Southern families. Here is the story in detail of such a feud, from its beginning to the present time [1888].

The trouble all began over two long-nosed, razor-backed, elm-peeler hogs. Randolph McCoy, known as Old Rand'l', is the head of the McCoy faction, and Anderson Hatfield, commonly called Bad Anse, is the head of the Hatfields. McCoy lived on the Blackberry Branch of Pond Creek, in Pike County, and Anse on the Logan County side of Tug River. Both men had a number of brothers, and every one of each family had just as many children as the laws of nature would permit.

One of Anse's brothers, Floyd by name, lived in Kentucky, near Randolph McCoy. The McCoy boys say that Floyd Hatfield "took up" two hogs that belonged to their father, Randolph McCoy. The Hatfields say that old Randolph took up two belonging to Floyd Hatfield, and the chances are, from what Randolph's own neighbors and friends tell of him, that he was the aggressor. The case came on for trial before Justice of the Peace Matthew Hatfield, and Floyd Hatfield had several witnesses who swore positively to the identity of the hogs, which were there present in court, tethered under a big beech tree near the house of the Justice. Randolph McCoy could bring no witnesses, and, of course, lost his suit and was obliged to pay costs. He went home very much disgruntled, but did nothing worse than talking for a couple of years.

However, Randolph's talk eventually brought on bloodshed. Among the witnesses in the suit over the hogs was old Bill Stayton. Bill was a brother of Floyd Hatfield's wife. It happened one day that Floyd Hatfield, Deacon Ellison Hatfield (Floyd's brother), young Bill Stayton, and several other members of the Hatfield family, were drawing a seine in Tug River for fish, when Randolph McCoy and two of his boys came along. Randolph got to talking about the two hogs, and the Hatfields talked back, and in the end Randolph said that old Bill Stayton had deliberately perjured himself at the trial. At this Bill Stayton, Jr., who was a boy of about eighteen years, picked up a stone and threw it at Randolph with such good aim that he knocked the old man down. Thereupon the McCoy boys jumped on young Bill, and would have killed him had not Deacon Hatfield interfered.

Within six months young Bill Stayton was shot dead in the road on one of the Pike County creeks. He was waylaid by Parish and Sam McCoy, nephews of Randolph. They were young men who had been persuaded into making trouble for young Bill by their uncle, Randolph, the Hatfields say. They were arrested, tried, and acquitted for lack of evidence.

The absolute acquittal of the two McCoy boys made the Hatfields mad, as they say in that country. They concluded that no West Virginian could get justice in a Kentucky court in a capital case. At a subsequent election, held in Pike County, at which the Hatfields from West Virginia were present as workers for relatives living on the Kentucky side, Old Rand'l' and his sons and brothers happened to be working for the same person, and the result was that the candidate got the two families together over a jug of moonshine whisky. There was just enough of whisky to make every one mellow, and not enough to make any one ugly; and so the two families made peace and lived comfortably for several years thereafter. Had it not been for an entirely new cause of trouble no blood save that of poor Bill Stayton would, in all probability, have been shed.

This time a wayward girl was at the bottom of the trouble. Pretty Rose Ann McCoy, a daughter of Old Rand'l', loved stalwart Johnson Hatfield, a son of Bad Anse. Rose Ann was twenty years old, and Johnson (now known only as Jonce) was eighteen. Rose Ann was old enough to know better, but she allowed Jonce to persuade her that a marriage tie was in no way necessary to the consummation of love. The girl's father and brothers knew that she occasionally met Jonce, but they supposed that it was an innocent courtship. The knowledge of the truth came to them somewhat rudely.

Jonce was an outlaw in Kentucky. He had been indicted at that time, although but eighteen years old, twenty-seven times. The crimes, however, were not venal in either Kentucky or West Virginia eyes. He had merely made a practice of bringing the moonshine whisky, which his father distilled in the mountain back of his home over to Kentucky, and selling it. He never entered Kentucky except at the risk of his liberty, and it was his bravado in thus defying the officers of the law that first attracted Rose Ann McCoy.

But as the indictments accumulated, and the prospects of large fines increased, Sheriff Joe Radcliffe, of Pike County, became anxious to capture the rascal, and offered a reward for his arrest, and made Talbot McCoy, son of Old Rand'l', a deputy.

So Talbot, having secured the warrant, bided his time until his sister, Rose Ann, made her usual excuse about going to see a neighbor down on Pond Creek. Talbot knew that the neighbor was none other than Jonce. After Rose Ann had gone, Talbot and his brother, Farmer, followed at a proper distance, and finally saw her leave the Pond Creek road and go up the dry bed of a small waterway, called in this county a "dreen." They then went up the mountain, and very cautiously descended the drain until on turning a clump of bushes, they surprised their sister with her lover.

In the eyes of the mountain folks along Tug River this sight was enough to make the boys "right mad," but it was not a case for blood.

As for Rose Ann, she cut around the mountain to the house of a friend, where she "borrowed a mule, and mounting it bareback, she rode at a full gallop to the river, which she forded, and then ran the mule to Anse Hatfield's house, Jonce's home, and told what had happened to Jonce.

It took but half an hour for Anse to gather a few neighbors and his own sons, and with guns and pistols loaded, start to rescue Jonce. This occurred in 1880. At the home of Old Rand'l', in Pikeville, is a bright boy of seven. He bears the name of McCoy, after his mother. Rose Ann. His father was Jonce Hatfield. In the fight on last New Year's night, in which the house of Old Rand'l' was burned and his son and daughter shot, this boy escaped death at the hands of his father by the thickness of a piece of muslin.

Rose Ann, after alarming the Hatfields in order that Jonce might be rescued, did not dare to return home, and so remained in the family of Bad Anse, living as the mistress of Jonce, without protest on the part of even Jonce's mother. Jonce and the girl slept in a bed in the same room with the old folks and several other members of the family. It is the custom of the country. Within a year, however, Jonce, who is a surly brute, turned her and her child, who was born in Virginia, away, and she has since lived with her father and mother.

"There were no open hostilities, even on her return," said a lawyer in Pikeville who was familiar with the story, "but, of course, the McCoys were mad."

During the year 1881 and the first half of 1882 the McCoys and the Hatfields kept away from each other.

CHAPTER 2

At the August election in 1882, in Pike County, Mr. Thomas Stafford was the candidate of the Democratic party for Justice of the Peace. Stafford was a brother-in-law of Elias, Valentine, Ellison, and Bad Anse Hatfield. He was also related by marriage to the McCoys. To insure Stafford's election the Hatfield brothers came over to Kentucky to use their influence on friends and acquaintances. The McCoys also turned out to aid Mr. Stafford.

But, as in the former reconciliation, the angel of peace was perched on the shoulders of the Democratic candidate, and she had a jug containing just the right quantity of moonshine in her hand. She held the jug to the lips of the Hatfields and the McCoys with impartial hand, and before noon had arrived past difficulties were forgotten and the boom for Stafford had swelled to magnificent proportions. All doubts of his election by a handsome majority were gone. It was an occasion to be celebrated by both Hatfields and McCoys. To celebrate it they sent for more moonshine Joe Davis kept a big supply of it at the mouth of Blackberry Creek, half a mile or so from where the election was held. Messengers were sent down to Joe's for whisky. It was brought in bottles. Part of it was apple moonshine and part was corn.

It is said regretfully now by those who were present that Joe Davis ought never to have sold both apple and corn moonshine, for the mixture always did and always will provoke men to wrath. Those who try the mixture for the first time say do they not doubt this statement.

However, it happened that between drinks Talbot McCoy met with that Elias Hatfield who is known as Bad 'Lias, to distinguish him from his uncle, Elias, the brother of Anse Valentine, and of Floyd, his father. Bad 'Lias had once borrowed $1.75 cash from Talbot McCoy, and had failed to return it as promised. Talbot wanted the money to buy moonshine with, and asked for it. 'Lias declared he did not owe Talbot a cent. Talbot jumped on him to pound him into paying the money. Talbot was a stalwart for a Kentucky mountaineer, and was rapidly beating 'Lias into submission when Ellison and Elias, the boy's uncles, came up. Elids had a revolver in his hand, and Ellison a pocketknife of large size, with the big blade open. Farmer McCoy also drew a pistol. Seeing them coming, Constable Matthew Hatfield, a Pike County officer, distantly related to the Virginia Hatfields, arrested Talbot McCoy and another constable arrested Bad 'Lias.

Unfortunately for all concerned, the mixture of two kinds of moonshine had so worked on the mind of good Deacon Ellison Hatfield that he was not now a peacemaker, as he had tried to be on a former occasion. Instead, he was dead in earnest in seeking for a fight. He reckoned the McCoys had come there for a fight, and he was ready to accommodate them. The biggest of the McCoys had pitched on little 'Lias, and nobody but a coward would do that. If the big McCoy was a man, he wouldn't stand there pretending that the constable was holding him, but would jump out and show what he could do with a man after making a beginning on a boy.

With each sentence the Deacon got more excited, and waved his knife closer to the body of Talbot McCoy. Seeing that Talbot was likely to be stabbed unless released (for on account of the pressure of the crowd about them, Constable Matthew Hatfield was unable to get his prisoner away), the constable released McCoy.

The moment he felt himself free, Talbot leaped back two jumps in the open ring the eager mountaineers had formed, and drew a pocket knife, much like that held by the Deacon. Then the two men sprang at each other on murder intent, while the crowd around surged and waved to and fro as each spectator strove to see every move that was made. The men met with a thud, and Talbot sank his knife into the Deacon's side, missing a fatal wound only because the point of the blade struck a rib and glanced. The Deacon gashed his opponent over the head, cutting through the soft felt hat, and clear to the skull, from the left ear over to the top of the forehead above the nose.

Then the two men separated by a step each, and here and there in a ring of spectators knives and revolvers appeared. In a moment the combatants came together again, and Ellison Hatfield's blade closed on his hand, cutting it, till he dropped the knife and started in to clean out Talbot with his fists. He was a more powerful man even than Talbot, or at least better as a wrestler, and was soon getting the best of the fight. But Talbot was as quick with the knife as an Italian desperado, and plunged it repeatedly into the Deacon's sides and hips. Some of the wounds were deadly, but in the heat of the fight the Deacon apparently did not notice them. It was alleged by the Hatfields, that two of the McCoys helped Talbot, by giving Ellison a sly stab as the two fighters surged first against one side of the ring of spectators, and then against another. Even little Budd McCoy, a lad of nine, is said to have stabbed Ellison twice in the legs, although Randolph, Jr., a lad of thirteen, was arrested for it at the time.

As Talbot's head struck the ground, Ellison grabbed a jagged stone, in lieu of the knife he had lost, and, raising it on high, was about to crush in the skull of his prostrate enemy, when Farmer McCoy, unable longer to restrain himself, fired his revolver full at Ellison's back. The bullet struck the Deacon just above the right suspender button, and ranged forward and upward, and he fell over unable to continue the fight.

Farmer McCoy dropped his pistol and fled up the road, while Elias opened fire with the pistol he had all the time carried in his hand. Farmer increased his pace as Elias fired, and all five chambers of the revolver were emptied in vain. Then Elias dropped his pistol and started after the fugitive, together with Constable Matthew Hatfield. Farmer was overtaken after a race of only about two hundred yards, and brought back to the big beech tree where the voting had been done.

The officers of the law had once more asserted themselves. Talbot and Farmer were both formally arrested, together with Randolph McCoy, Jr., who with a companion, had been playing at a spring a quarter of a mile away until the firing began, and came running up just as Farmer was brought back to the polling place. He was accused of cutting the Deacon in the legs by a Hatfield who mistook him for the young boy, Budd. This fact is now admitted on all sides, but the McCoys deny that Budd did any stabbing, and say that Talbot did it all.

When the McCoys were arrested they were taken to the house of John Hatfield for the night, as it was by this time late in the afternoon, and there guarded until morning.

The Deacon was put on a rude stretcher made with quilts and poles, and carried to the house of Terrall.

The doctor found twenty-seven cuts in various parts of the deacon's body, including one in the side that split the right lung. The course of the bullet could not be traced.

The news of the shooting spread along the river and up the creeks and branches on both sides, like an autumn fire up a mountainside, and when morning came there were over seventy of the Hatfield family from West Virginia about the house of John Hatfield on Blackberry Creek, where the prisoners were kept over night. The majority of the McCoys, following the example set by Old Rand'l' himself, flunked.

After daylight appeared on Tuesday, the prisoners and their guards ate breakfast and set out for Pikesville jail. They had not traveled over a mile, however, before they met a gang of West Virginia Hatfields headed by old Bad Anse Hatfield, brother of Ellison. Anse's son Jonce was along. All were armed. Anse said he wanted the boys taken to the mouth of Blackberry Creek for trial, so that the testimony of Dr. Rutherford could be taken without keeping him so long from the side of Ellison as would be necessary were the trial to be held as proposed. The prisoners as well as the rest concerned, agreed to go to the mouth of Blackberry Creek except Justice Joseph Hatfield. All ate dinner at Anderson Hatfield's, and then Bad Anse called his party of West Virginians to one side, out in the yard. They had a consultation there, after which Bad Anse called out in a loud voice:

"All friends of the Hatfields fall in line, two and two."

About forty men fell into line, but at the request of Anderson Hatfield the line was formed outside of his yard. Then Bad Anse called for a rope, and Charley Carpenter, one of Anse's crowd, brought one from his horse. It had been obtained at the house of Jerry Hatfield, another Kentuckian, by Anse, on his way up Blackberry Creek before he met the prisoners on their way to jail. Carpenter then tied the prisoners together by their arms. When the prisoners had been tied Carpenter took hold of the end of the line and drove them before him like animals into the road. Then Bad Anse nodded to Justice Hatfield and said: "We will take charge."

The boys were driven to a ford near where William McCoy lives, and across into West Virginia. Then they were driven to a log schoolhouse, and there confined under a guard heavily armed. They reached the schoolhouse in the middle of Tuesday afternoon. Here they were at first told they would have a trial on Wednesday afternoon, with Justice Wall Hatfield, who had been a ringleader in kidnapping them from Kentucky, as presiding Judge; but all pretense that they were to be tried lawfully was soon thrown aside. Bad Anse settled that as soon as the mother of the prisoners came to the schoolhouse. The mother knelt down before Anse, and with hands clasped and voice choked with sobs, begged him to allow her boys to have a fair trial under the law.

"Yo' needn't beg and yo' needn't cry," said Anse. "If Ellison dies, yo' boys has got to die."

Talbot was a married man, and had a girl baby four months old. The wife came about the time his mother arrived, and she, too, with her child in her arms, went on her knees to Anse and to Wall. It was useless.

The treatment of the prisoners during the time that they were kept awaiting the death of Ellison was atrocious. They had been tied together with a heavy rope on Tuesday, immediately after dinner, the rope being drawn so tight around their arms as to prevent the circulation of the blood. Not for a moment was this rope loosened.

In addition to the torture of the rope the prisoners were constantly reminded of their fate by their captors. Justice Wall frequently said to them that prayer to the Almighty was not only a duty, but a pleasure in time of tribulation, and said that it would not hurt them even should Ellison's recovery permit them to escape death. The Hatfield boys and their friends discussed the points of the human form in which a bullet would produce the greatest pain, and jeered whenever the prisoners said anything.

It was half a mile from the schoolhouse to the mouth of the creek where Ellison was dying, in Anderson Ferrall's house. Messengers passed to and fro frequently. Bad Anse and Wall occasionally visited their brother, while Elias remained with him almost continually. They asked him what should be done with the prisoners in case he died, and he replied: "Give them the civil law."

Finally, at three o'clock the wounded man breathed his last, and Dr. Rutherford told the mourners that he was dead. The deacon was a married man, and had several children. The widow and the orphans knelt around the bed and wept aloud, and the dead man's brothers, Elias and Anse, who were present, went out in the yard and refused to speak to any one. A messenger jumped on a mule and rode in a gallop to the schoolhouse with the news. A great cry arose as he shouted that "Ellison's done died," and a number of the guards began running around the schoolhouse and peering in through the chinks between the logs to find a place from which they could shoot at the prisoners without hitting their own friends.

The prisoners, knowing now that their fate was determined, broke down and wept, but Talbot very soon recovered his composure, and made one last appeal.

"Gentlemen," he said, "when you shoot me I want you to look me in the face: Don't go behind me."

As night came on Anse mustered the following gang of men: Jonce Hatfield, Cap. Hatfield (both his own sons), Valentine and Elias Hatfield (brothers), Charley Carpenter, Joseph Murphy, Bill Tom Hatfield, Doc. Mayhom, Plyant Mayhorn, Selkirk McCoy and his sons Albert and L. D., Thomas Mitchell, Lark Varny, Andy Varny, Daniel Whitt, Sam Mayhorn, Alex. Messer, John Whitt, and Ellison Mounts. Having formed them in line before the schoolhouse, with a sort of military orders he had learned when a bushwacker, he detailed Charley Carpenter to bring out the prisoners. They were driven along toward Kentucky, with no one saying a word. Farmer and Little Randolph McCoy were crying. Sam Simpkins, who kept a store at the mouth of the creek (Mate), saw them go by, and recognized them in the faint light^ of the stars. As they entered the water to wade across, Farmer fainted from fear and exhaustion, and was dragged across by two of the gang. The lad wept louder than ever, but Talbot marched erect and in silence, man fashion.

CHAPTER 3

At that moment James McCoy, the brother of the prisoners, stood in the yard of his uncle, Asa, a third of a mile up, and on the Virginia side of the river which the gang had just crossed. It was a perfectly quiet night, and he heard the gang cross the river, and knew that the end was near. Slipping out he ran down the river a short distance in the cover of some bushes, but could see nothing, for the Kentucky bank of the river is covered with trees. He waited a few minutes, and then a voice was heard from the Kentucky side about a quarter of a mile up from where the boys had crossed, which said:

"All ready."

Then the voice of Wall Hatfield, from the Virginia side, was heard saying: "Take aim. Fire!"

There was a roar of guns and pistols. Jim could see the flashes under the trees distinctly. Several shots were fired after the first volley, and then all was still for two minutes. Then came the wail of a boy's voice followed by the heavy report of a double-barreled shotgun.

When the gang reached the Kentucky side they stopped, and by dashing water into Farmer's face, revived him that he might suffer the more. Then they forced the prisoners along the grassy bank under the trees, until a slight depression was reached. Here were a number of pawpaw trees. The prisoners were there thrown to the ground, and then raised on their knees, and each one tied in that position to a pawpaw bush. Talbot, who had asked to be shot in the face, was tied with his back to his executioners; but Farmer, who was already nearly dead with fear, was tied facing them. The lad was tied facing his brothers, and then the gang formed in line, and Bad Anse shouted to Wall, who was on the other side of the river, for the word. As it came they all fired, and the two older brothers, Talbot and Farmer, fell dead. The crying of the lad had ceased through horror and fear. After a few shots had been fired into the dead bodies by Cap and Jonce Hatfield, Ellison Mounts, and Tom Mitchell, to gratify their innate thirst for the safe shedding of blood, the gang started down the river. But fear overcame one of their number, Alex Messer, and he said:

"Dead men tell no tales."

He referred to the lad who had recognized them all.

"Go you," said Bad Anse, and Messer loaded his shotgun with rifle balls, and going back, leveled it at the head of the boy. The lad saw him and gave one cry, and then both barrels were fired together. The entire top of the boy's head was blown away, and a piece of his skull, four inches across, was picked up ten feet away up the sloping bank next day. His body did not fall, but remained kneeling until found by the Coroner.

As the gang marched back to West Virginia, Justice of the Peace, Valentine Hatfield (Wall), met them. Bad Anse formed them in line facing the Justice.

"Hold up your right hands," said Wall, and all obeyed.

"You and each of you do solemnly swear never to reveal to any one what has been done this night under the penalty of death, so help your God. Each say, 'I do.' "

The men who fired into the McCoy boys were Anse, Cap, and Jonce Hatfield, Charley Carpenter, Tom Mitchell,

Doc Mayhorn, Joe Murphy, Bill Tom Hatfield, Alex Messer, and Ellison Mounts.

On Thursday morning, Justice of the Peace, Joseph Hatfield, acting as Coroner, cut the ropes that bound the bodies to the pawpaws, and a jury of twelve men solemnly inspected the work of the West Virginians, and brought in a verdict that the boys had "come to their death by shot wounds at the hands of persons to the jury unknown." It took nearly half an hour for the Coroner and his jury to perform this legal duty.

Then Jim McCoy and his brother Sam and the Justice of the Peace carried the bodies up the hillside a few rods to the road and placed them on a narrow sled drawn by oxen. While they did this, someone unknown carved with a jack-knife in the smooth bark of a big beech tree, whose limbs shaded the spot where the tragedy occurred, this inscription, with a rude border around it:

THE McCOY BOYS
Shot in 1882

The funeral was held that afternoon at the home of old Randolph, near the head of the Blackberry Fork of Pond Creek. More than one thousand people came, and over nine hundred horses and mules were "hanged to the trees and bushes "up and down the road and about a large yard that surrounded McCoy's house. A wide grave was dug on a small tableland that jutted out from the side of the mountain that rose on the northerly side of the brook opposite old Randolph's house. Then kindly neighbors placed the bodies in coffins on a litter and carried them across the brook and up the slope to the grave. Here the old mother fell on her knees, as the Baptist preacher who conducted the services was about to begin his prayer, and called on God to witness that had her pleading been listened to on the morning of election neither Ellison nor her boys had suffered cruel and cowardly deaths.

CHAPTER 4

Talbot's widow was left with quite a little property for a mountaineer's wife. Talbot was a timber dealer as well as farmer, and had quite an interest in rafts of logs. His widow "was rascaled out of a heap of it," as Floyd McCoy said, by Talbot's partner, but she still had enough to make her comfortable and provide for the girl baby in a land where the comforts of life consist of "corn, pone and bacon," and the luxuries of hot biscuit and honey. But the unfortunate woman was not to be comforted by any inheritance. She had been a happy, hearty, handsome wife, according to the accounts of friend and foe. But the grave had not closed over her dead husband before she "began to look puny." She wept less than her mother-in-law, with whom she came to live. She would even, when the old lady would stop her work to clasp her hands and fall on the floor and cry aloud over the fate of her sons, soothe and comfort her instead of weeping, too. But she could not sleep at night because the roar of those guns was ever in her ears, and from day to day she was less able to do the work required of a woman on a farm. Eventually she was unable to leave her bed, and finally died, literally of a broken heart.

But while the McCoys, if in any way affected, were simply cowed by the murder of the three boys, the Hatfields were incited to further deeds.

"Anse he's got some boys thet's mighty mean. Anse can't do nothin' with 'em, and never could. Cap, he's gin us trouble ever sence he was table high. They've went on and carried on till I don't blame the authorities for tryin' to punish sech triflin' fellers."

That is what Elias Hatfield, brother of Bad Anse, and one of the murderers of the three McCoys, had to say about Anse's boys when asked for a history of the feud.

In June 1884 an attempt was made to kill both Randolph McCoy and his son Calvin, that resulted in maiming for life two inoffensive citizens through a curious mistake.

It will be remembered that the killing of the good Deacon Hatfield occurred at an election when brother-in-law Tom Stafford was candidate for Justice of the Peace. Of course Tom was elected.

Now, when Talbot's estate was settled, Calvin looked after the interests of the widow, and was obliged to bring several suits to establish her rights. It some way happened that the Logan Regulators heard when one of these suits was to have a hearing, and accordingly, knowing that both old Rand'l' and Calvin would be present, formed a plan to kill them both. Cap and Jonce Hatfield, Mose Christian, Lee Wilson, Ellison Mounts, Harvey Smith, and Bill Tom Hatfield took guns and hid themselves in the brush on the mountain side a few rods above the road over which the McCoys would travel when going home after the trial.

Once their ambush was fixed, the little son of Justice Stafford was seen passing along the road, and Cap stopped him and made him bring an accurate description of the dress and arms of both Randolph McCoy and Calvin.

But the boy overlooked one circumstance. Two of the witnesses at the trial, John and Hense Scott, happened to be not only dressed as were Randolph and Calvin McCoy, but they had beards of the same cut and color.

The sun had gone down behind a mountain when the trial was over, and the parties to the trial filed out. The first to come were the Scotts. They, with Sam McCoy, son of Randolph, started down the road before the rest appeared. The bushwhackers supposed they had three of the McCoys before them, and as they got opposite the ambush fired. One ball pierced John Scott's right knee, and he fell to the ground. Another ploughed through Hense Scott's right shoulder directly under Sam McCoy's hand. Sam felt the flesh and clothing rise under his hand as the bullet cut through the flesh and bones. Hense and Sam jumped over the bank, down below the road (a mere bridle path) and got out of sight, while John had to lie there in the dust exposed to the fire of the bushwhackers. He closed his eyes and lay as still as possible while the balls cut and ploughed up the dirt of the road on both sides of him until he was covered with it. Fortunately no other ball struck him.

Among the Regulators, as already mentioned, was Tom Wallace. Tom had married a daughter of Bill Daniels, who lived on the Kentucky side of Tug River. Tom was so ugly to his wife, that she was obliged to leave him and return home. Some time after this, when a raid was contemplated by the Hatfields, the news of it got to the McCoys, so that they fled. Cap Hatfield and Tom Wallace at once concluded that Mrs. Daniels and her daughter, Tom's wife, had betrayed the Regulators. So one night, Tom and Cap crossed Tug River to the Daniels' cabin. No one ever locks a door in that country unless concerned in a feud, and the Daniels' door was not even latched. Tom and Cap pushed it open and walked in. The whole family was in bed—all, of course, in the one room. A pile of soft coal blazed in the fireplace.

Bill Daniels awoke as the intruders strode across the floor. Bill found the muzzle of a cocked repeating rifle in his face as he opened his eyes. It was held by Tom Wallace, and he was told to lie still and say nothing.

Then Cap ordered Mrs. Daniels and Mrs. Wallace, her daughter, out of bed. The women obeyed, but began to cry and plead for mercy, at which Cap laughed in glee. He carried in his hand the tail of a cow, which he cut from an unfortunate brute some time before, just to see her jump, and had then hung it up and dried it. He flourished this about his head, and then, grabbing Mrs. Daniels by the hair, forced her to her knees in front of the fire-place, and began beating her across the back, using the heavy bone end of the cow's tail to strike her with. The blows were delivered with a will. The woman screamed in agony, for the first two blows broke two ribs, while to her cries were added those of her daughter and several children. Bill Daniels, the husband and father, groaned and turned his head, but Tom ordered him under pain of death to turn back and keep his eyes on the whipping.

From Mrs. Daniels Cap turned to Mrs. Wallace, her daughter. His arm was somewhat weary now, and he could not beat her to his satisfaction, so he took the gun from Wallace, who, with fresh strength, beat the woman anew. The actual beating lasted over forty minutes by a little old clock that stood over the fireplace on a shelf. When it was over both women lay on the floor unconscious—dead, Daniels supposed, though Mrs. Daniels afterward partially recovered, and Mrs. Wallace is in good health now. Mrs. Daniels' lungs were affected, and she will probably die of consumption inside of a year.

CHAPTER 5

There are two stories of the murder that followed this assault. The McCoys tell this:

Mrs. Daniels was a sister of Jeff McCoy, who was a cousin of Randolph's boys. Some time after Mrs. Daniels had been beaten Bad Anse met Jeff McCoy in the road and greeted him in a friendly way. Jeff had never taken any part in the feud, and had always been well treated by both sides. Anse said he was mighty sorry about the beating Mrs. Daniels had got, and that Cap was making him a heap of trouble. But Cap was his own boy, and a father must stand by his son. There was no reason for standing by Tom Wallace, however, and if Jeff would like to get even with his ornery pictures Anse was the man to help the matter on. Jeff was profuse in his thanks, and it was agreed that Jeff should go over to Anse's house, that Tom should be invited there and given over to Jeff, who should then escort him to Pikeville jail and have him sent to the penitentiary. The plan worked well up to the meeting of Jeff and Wallace, which happened at Jonce Hatfield's home, on Grapevine Creek. Then the program was changed. Jeff was made the prisoner of Tom Wallace, and tied with a rope to Tom Wallace's saddle and driven like a pig down Grapevine Creek to Cap Hatfield's house. It is said that Cap nearly laughed himself sick when he saw Jeff driven into his yard and learned how neatly the old man had worked on the unsophisticated mind of McCoy. When he had recovered his composure, however, he got down the repeating rifle and told Tom to drive the victim down the road until opposite the Daniels cabin. There they could kill him in sight of his sister.

Cap lived at the mouth of Grapevine Creek, on the bank of Tug River. One mile below, at the mouth of Thacker Creek, lived Shang Bill Ferrall. At Shang's house the two men, with their prisoner, stopped, in order that Cap might get a drink. Jeff saw a chance to slip the rope from the horn of Tom's saddle, and did so, and in a moment had jumped the low fence around Shang's yard and plunged headlong from an eight-foot bank into the river. He escaped to the Kentucky shore with only a flesh wound in his left arm. But once on shore he lost his head. First he sought refuge behind a bush that could scarce have sheltered a rabbit. Then he fled when that grew too hot up the bare mountainside, straight away from the enemy, when he might have run down the river and in six jumps gained a big oak and plenty of big beech trees. He had crossed nearly half the open space, however, when a ball from Cap's gun killed him.

According to the Hatfields, Jeff had stabbed a neighbor and fled to Virginia for a harbor. Anse and Jonce agreed to take him in, but Cap opposed it. Jeff was at Jonce's house three weeks, Jonce having married Jeff's sister. Then Jeff went down to Cap's house and got into a quarrel with Tom Wallace, whom he met there, and shot Tom, inflicting a slight wound. Cap then arrested Jeff, and was taking him to a justice when he escaped.

The death of Jeff McCoy led to the first efforts worthy of the name to bring the Hatfields to trial for their crimes. Jeff was a nephew of Perry Cline, a leading lawyer of Pike.

Lawyer Cline set about getting rewards offered for the

arrest of the murderers, not only of Jeff McCoy, but of Talbot, Farmer, and little Randolph McCoy. A hundred dollars each was the sum offered. Two of Jeff's brothers, Budd and Jake, heard that Wallace was working on the extension of the railroad along the Big Sandy, and went down there and got him. He was in Pikeville jail four weeks, and then, one night when a son of Perry Cline carried food to the prisoners, Cline being jailer, the boy was overpowered, and all hands escaped, including John C. McCoy, who was in for a stabbing not in any way connected with the feud.

The escape of Tom incited Perry Cline to further efforts, and application was made to Governor Willis Wilson, of West Virginia, for a requisition for the indicted men. Up to this time politics had had nothing to do with the feud, but it now entered in.

In the office of the Secretary of State of West Virginia, was one John B. Floyd, a nephew of the member of President Buchanan's Cabinet of that name. Floyd aspired to be his party's candidate for Governor, and to that end wished to have his county solid behind him. His home was in Logan County, and he knew the Hatfields personally. They are a most prolific race, and were powerful political workers in the mountains. Floyd heard of the application to Governor Wilson, and sent word to the Hatfields. Under his instructions, they got up a petition, saying that they were peaceful mountain farmers, who had been greatly oppressed and abused by the relatives of a Kentucky desperado, named Randolph McCoy, and praying that the Governor would not further the ends of the Kentucky villain by giving them over to be tried. The Hatfield Regulators rode up and down the creeks, and branches of half of Logan County, carrying their repeating rifles and the petition. Every man met signed the petition.

Nevertheless, Governor Wilson was for a time persuaded to issue a requisition. While negotiations pended, Governor Buckner offered five hundred dollars each, for

Bad Anse, Cap, and Jonce Hatfield, Tom Mitchell (under the name of Chambers), and Tom Wallace. Along in October, 1887, Governor Wilson wrote to County Attorney Lee Ferguson, of Pike County, saying, that if fifty-two dollars was sent to pay expenses incurred by Clerk John B. Floyd, while investigating the case, papers for the arrest of all the indicted men, save Elias and Wall Hatfield, and Andy Varney, would be issued.

At this stage, a new man became involved in the feud, and he has since become the object of the most deadly hatred of the Hatfields, and the contempt of even the McCoys, yet he is protected in Pike County. It was Deputy Sheriff Frank Phillips. He was appointed State agent for Kentucky to receive West Virginia prisoners. Phillips sent on a part of the fifty-two dollars demanded by Governor Wilson, and asked for the papers for Cap, Jonce, and Anse Hatfield, and Tom Mitchell, who, however, was called Tom Chambers in the indictment. Tom was born out of wedlock, and one Tom Chambers subsequently married his mother, so he was called both Chambers and Mitchell. The error in the papers led to the arrest of his stepfather.

Without waiting for the arrival of the papers, which by the way never came, Phillips, with Jim and Sam McCoy, sons of Randolph, started over to Virginia to bring in the four Logan men named, or any other indicted men they could find. They supposed Tom Chambers, the stepfather of Tom Mitchell, was the one of the four wanted. They got to Tom's house at eleven o'clock on the night of Dec. 9, 1887. Tom was in bed. A bright coal fire burned on the hearth within, and a bright and unusually large bulldog stood guard outside. The three men dismounted, with Sam at the front door and Jim and Phillips at the rear. Jim broke in the rear door, and at the same moment the bulldog took a grip on Phillips' thigh. Phillips shot the dog with one revolver and held another on Chambers and made him surrender.

The next raid was made on Dec. 20. Frank Phillips, Jim

McCoy, and his cousin Budd, the murdered Jeff McCoy's brother, went up in McDowell County, West Virginia, and found Selkirk McCoy and Mose Christian in a little cross-roads store near Perryville and brought them safely to Pikeville jail. These two raids incited the Hatfields to a sort of revenge that horrified the people not only of both counties, but every one else that ever heard the story. Even Bad Anse himself has talked against it.

CHAPTER 6

On New Year's night of this year there were at Randolph's house besides himself and wife, his son Calvin and Rose Ann's little boy Melvin, all of whom were in the westerly end of the house. In the other end were Allaphare, Addie, and Fanny McCoy, daughters of Randolph and young women grown, besides little Cora, the orphan daughter of Talbot.

Shortly after midnight they were awakened by a gang of Hatfields, who called on old Rand'l' to surrender or they would burn his house over his head. The gang was headed by Uncle Jim Vance, who had hitherto kept out of the trouble and was got into it by a circumstance which illustrates the morals of these mountaineers very well, but the story of which must be told at another time. Uncle Jim's sister was the wife of Bad Anse.

With Vance were Cap Hatfield, Jonce Hatfield, Bob Hatfield, a younger son of Cap; Elliott Hatfield, son of Ellison; Ellison Mounts, an illegitimate son of the dead Deacon; French Ellis, Tom Gillespie, and Tom Mitchell.

Gillespie and Elliott Hatfield were posted up and down the road. The other seven attacked the house.

Old Rand'l' made no answer to the demand to surrender, and an effort was made to break in his door. The door was barred. Then the gang attacked the other end, where the girls were, and broke in their door, and jumped back lest a man should be inside and shoot out.

Allaphare, the oldest girl, went to the door and told them no man was in there.

"Stir a light," ordered Jim Vance, and Allaphare went to the fireplace and tried to build a fire. But the coal was out, and there was neither wood nor match to light a fire. Allaphare returned to the door and told the men why she could make no fire. The men broke out in a torrent of profanity, and Cap Hatfield swore he would shoot her if she did not at once make afire in the fireplace. She recognized his voice, and said, bursting into tears:

"Cap, I can't; I would, indeed I would, if I could. You wouldn't shoot a woman who never did you any harm, would you?"

"What the ——— are you parleying with her for?" yelled Uncle Jim. "God ——— her, make no more account of her than you would of a man. Shoot her, ——— her."

Cap raised his gun, but Ellison Mounts had his gun already at his shoulder, and shot the girl down as she stood there in her nightgown. The ball entered just over the left breast, and she fell back dead with only a moan.

Then one of the gang who had found a bag of cotton between the two houses, brought a handful of it, set it on fire, and threw it into the room. By its light they could see that no man was concealed in the room, and they were, therefore, safe to put all their forces on the other end.

A part of them had already been engaged there. They had shot the southerly door to pieces, so that a determined rush would have broken it open, but a rush of that sort was what no Hatfield has the courage to make.

One of the gang, however, brought burning cotton and piled it against the door, but Mrs. McCoy had been churning the night before and had four gallons of buttermilk in churn. The old man took a tin cup and sitting down near the door dipped milk on the fire with one hand and held a revolver ready to shoot with the other.

Then they tried to fire the roof. Tom Mitchell climbed up the logs, and with one hand over the top log held a blazing torch against the clapboards. The old man saw the hand, and putting his revolver as close to it as possible, shot all four fingers off close to the knuckle. Cap tells gleefully to this day how Tom "cried like a baby over the loss of his fingers."

Calvin had not been idle all this time. He had mounted to the attic, and, kicking off the gable boards, and here and there a clapboard from the roof, had opened port holes through which he got several shots at the gang. One ball passed lengthwise through Ellison Mount's left forearm, soon after he had killed Allaphare, but it was from a .32-caliber rifle, and did not make a permanent injury. However, Calvin drove the gang under the porch on the south side of his end of the building, and between the buildings, and there they were secure. Calvin kicked off roof boards, and strove to remove a part of the roof of the porch, but in vain. From their retreat under the porch the gang kept up a fire on the door, and, at the same time kept applying torches to the house roof, while one or two others fired the roof successfully at the end where the girls were, and it began to get very warm for Calvin.

While the men were fighting, the old mother of the murdered girl had taken advantage of the lull in the shooting to slip out of the door facing the road to go around where the girls were. She had heard the other girls scream that Allaphare had been shot. As she went out the door Jonce Hatfield fired at a form on the bed, and the bullet cut the quilt over his own son. This story is told by the Hatfield crowd as one of the jokes of the feud. It would have been a good one of Jonce, Cap says, if he killed his own whelp.

Mrs. McCoy started around to the door of the other part of the house. As she passed the space between the houses, Jim Vance ordered her back with an oath, and raised his gun with a threat to shoot her.

"I saw it was wrong end to for that," Mrs. McCoy said when telling of it, "and kept on. But he struck me in the side with it and knocked me down. It broke two ribs. Pretty soon I got on my hands and knees. I felt so weak I couldn't get up, and so crawled on. Some one with a pistol got before me. 'For the Lord's sake, let me go to my girl,' I said. 'Go back, —— you, or I'll kill you,' he said. 'Oh!' I said, 'she's dead. For the love of the Lord, let me go to her,' and then I put out my hand. I could almost touch her feet as she lay there, and I could see her blood where it had run out of the door. Oh! my God! my God!"

In her grief in telling of the horrors of that night, the mother forgets what happened to herself as she put out her hand. The man who stopped her was Jonce Hatfield, and he struck her a blow with his revolver on the head that drove the hammer to the skull and left her senseless. They supposed she was dead.

In was not long after this before the fire drove Calvin from the attic. He said to the old man that he should strive to reach a corn crib about one hundred yards away across the yard to the northwest. From that point he could cover the retreat of the old man, and both might then cross the fork and reach the woods.

With a box of cartridges in one hand and his rifle in the other Calvin leaped from the door and ran across the yard. As he cleared the corner of the house where the gang could see him they opened fire. It was a regular roar, and it roused the old man to action, and he followed.

Calvin was by this time seventy-five yards away, in the shadow of some trees, and almost safe, but a bullet pierced his brain and he fell dead unknown even to those who shot him.

The gang had spread out from their retreat at the west end of the house, where they had gone as Calvin came down the ladder, and as the old man sprang out he saw them before him, while they did not notice him. He leveled a double-barreled shotgun at Jonce Hatfield and shot him in the right shoulder, and Jonce fell. Then he saw Tom Mitchell before him and fired. The shot pierced Tom's cartridge belt and entered the flesh of the abdomen, but the wounds, on account of the thickness of the belt, were of little account.

Then the firing at the old man began, and he ran the best he could and escaped untouched. He reached the corn crib, and from thence passed on up the mountain on the other side of the fork to the woods. He was dressed in shirt and drawers only, and it was a very cold night. Had he not have been lucky enough to find some hogs sleeping against some hay in an old barn on the next farm, he would probably have died from exposure. He routed the hogs out and got into the bed they had left.

After the men had left the house and the firing ceased the girls Addie and Fanny, finding the roof falling in, ventured to leave the house. They saw the gang just turning a point of the mountain on the road to Tug River. Then they picked up their dead sister, and followed by the little orphan Cora, they dragged the body to the edge of the woods to the southeast of the house, and there built a fire and cowered down by it. Their mother had by this time revived enough to crawl after them as they drew the body of Allaphare away from the burning building. Little Malvin ran out at the time his grandfather did, and was clutching the old man's leg, but he tripped and fell at the door, and then crawled away around another corner of the house and was unnoticed. The women remained by the fire until morning without clothes or assistance.

On the morning of January 2, the family was cared for and sent to Pikeville. The old man and Jim and Sam came on ahead. The neighbors prepared Allaphare and Calvin for the grave, and buried them on the mountainside with their dead brothers. The graves are plainly seen from the road. They are surrounded by an old rail fence after the fashion of the country, and shaded by a peach tree that will not live to bear fruit another year.

The old farm is let to a tenant, and is going to ruin.

CHAPTER 7

The murder of Allaphare roused Pike County as it had not been roused since the Civil War. The mountaineers have chivalry, if not courage, and they were ready, after a fashion, to avenge the murder of a woman. Out of a host of volunteers Frank Phillips selected twenty-three men, and early on the morning of January 6 rode out of Pikeville to raid Logan County for indicted Logan Regulators. They reached Anse Hatfield's home, on the bank of Tug River, opposite the mouth of Peter Creek, at night. Of course Anse was not at home, but the women and children were, and they were terribly alarmed. Jim McCoy and five others stayed there that night, one keeping guard all the time, of course.

Next morning, very early, the mob went down to Thacker Creek, where Shang Ferrall lives, and took him along to prevent him from giving an alarm. Three miles up above Thacker lived Uncle Jim Vance, but when they reached the house no one was there. It is a remarkable fact that a trail of blood from the burned home of Old Rand'l' led down to Tug River, was found again on the east side, and 1 ended at Jim Vance's yard. The Kentuckians were able to trace the trail on the 6th quite easily.

From Vance's the mob started to go over on Mate Creek, following up a branch that was a shorter way than the regular road. At the head of the branch, and right in the gap of the mountain, they met old Mrs. Vance coming down with an empty pail in her hand. She had been carrying breakfast up to Uncle Jim and to Cap, who had slept in that mountain. As she saw the mob, she turned and shouted:

"Here they come."

"How many?" asked Uncle Jim.

"About forty, I reckon."

During this talk the Kentuckians had charged up past the woman.

Uncle Jim yelled "Halt!" and then shouted, "Charge 'em, boys! Rally, boys! Charge 'em!" and at the same time began to shoot.

The orders, except the first, were bluff, for there were no boys there to rally, except Cap Hatfield, who flunked and ran like a sheep with dogs after it. He did not even shoot one shot. But Uncle Jim was too old to run, and made a virtue of necessity. He dodged behind a locust stub still several feet high and eight inches thick, and, taking aim at Frank Phillips, who led the mob, fired. Phillips is a remarkable cool-headed desperado. Just as the old man got his gun to his face Phillips dropped to the ground, and the bullet passed harmlessly over his head. Then he jumped up and fired as he ran forward to gain the shelter of a tree; but the old man fired again, and again Phillips dodged. This seems almost incredible, but the story is told by both parties. After this shot Phillips gained the shelter of a big oak, and tried to get a shot at the old man from it. As he peered around, he saw the old man had the drop on him and dodged back just in time. The bullet knocked a shower of bark into Phillips's face. But at this same instant Phillips leveled his gun and fired square at the center of the stump that concealed the old man. The stump was partly rotten, and the ball passed through it, striking Uncle Jim's cartridge belt and knocking him away from his shelter. Before the old man could recover himself Phillips had pumped in a fresh cartridge and shot him through the body. Uncle Jim dropped to the ground behind a log, and Phillips ran forward, supposing the old man was done for. In truth he was fatally hurt, but he was game yet. He had drawn a revolver as he fell, and before Phillips had taken two steps he saw the old man peering over the log holding the pistol with both hands. Uncle Jim was afflicted with a sort of St. Vitus dance that made his eyes roll and his whole frame shake about, yet he was accounted the best pistol shot in Logan County. Phillips dropped the moment he saw the old man, and the old man shrunk down a bit too. That was a mistake, for it enabled Phillips to aim his rifle where the old man's head must appear as he raised to look for Phillips. In a moment the gray hairs on his forehead rose above the log and Phillips fired. The ball knocked the old man's hat ten feet away and scattered his brains over the leaves for a yard around. The old lady, his wife, saw him killed. Walking up to his body she said: "Pore ole man; he's dead," and then walked away. Uncle Jim had been neither a faithful nor a kind husband, and the widow shed no tears.

The killing of Uncle Jim ended that raid. The Kentucky mob did not develop a relish for blood. They returned to Kentucky, but on January 9 started on another raid. This time they went on Beech Creek, in Logan County. They reached the house of Justice Wall Hatfield at noon, and leaping their horses over the fence, charged on the house. Wall, instead of jumping for his gun, ran to the door to see what was the racket (as he supposed) with the cows. Jim McCoy covered him with a rifle, and the Justice threw up his hands. In the house the mob found Doc and Sam Mayhorn, who were wanted for killing the three McCoy boys. This made three prisoners. The mob went on up the creek, however, and found Plyant Mayhorn and Andy Varny, and then went over on another branch and got L.

D. McCoy. Andy Varny tried to escape, but Sam McCoy and Dave Stratton ran him down, instead of shooting him according to the custom.

The third and last raid was made beginning January 16. There were thirty-three men in the mob. On the 18th they reached West Virginia, opposite Peter Creek, and rode down along the bank of Tug River to the mouth of Grapevine Creek. Here lived Cap Hatfield. Jim McCoy was in advance of the rest of the mob, who had to ride along single file, of course, on account of the road being narrow. His horse was restive, and when within a short distance of the creek Jim let it go ahead on the run. Rounding a little spur of the mountain, Jim found himself riding square at thirteen of the Logan Regulators, who were in Cap's yard, guns in hand, waiting for the Kentuckians. Jim tried to rein in his horse, but at that instant the Regulators began firing, and the beast danced with fear. The dancing probably saved Jim's life, for it prevented fair aim.

Now, although no one else was in sight, the Regulators knew that others were behind Jim, and so stepped off to one side, where they could get better shelter behind a fence. Meantime Jim managed to get off of his horse and quiet the beast, although the bullets were whistling on all sides. Then Jim coolly laid his gun on the ground, pulled off his overcoat which was too tight for him, and placing it on the saddle, turned the horse loose. Then he picked up his gun, walked deliberately to a fence corner, and taking aim over it, fired. He brought his man down at the first shot. The man was Bill Dempsey. At that the other twelve Regulators turned and ran like sheep, with Cap Hatfield leading the way, although no other Kentuckian had come in sight save Budd McCoy, and he had been shot down by a bullet in his shoulder.

The Kentuckians gathered in Cap's yard, but could at first find no one there, although Jim, who did not go into the yard, had said he had shot one man. But a trail of blood was found that led into a shuck pen. There they found Bill Dempsey shot through the body.

"What is your name," said Frank Phillips.

"Bill Dempsey," said he, holding up his hands, "I am not armed, gentlemen, and am dying now. Please don't shoot me any more. Don't, don't."

The last words were uttered as he saw Phillips draw a revolver. Several of the mob saw the revolver, too, and jumped to catch it, but they were too late. Phillips shot the man through the head. That act ended the raiding business. It was especially bad for the Kentuckians, for Dempsey was there as a lawful police officer to arrest raiding parties.

But the raids had affected the Hatfields much, as the deeds of the Regulators had previously affected the McCoys, only worse. They immediately abandoned their farms, and moved over to Island Creek, in the neighborhood of Logan Court House, and here they are now. Jonce is in Colorado.

CHAPTER 8

It must not be supposed that no resort to legal proceedings was made by the West Virginians. The day that
the first man, Tom Chambers, was kidnapped, the law firm
of Auries, Ferrall & Connolly, of Pikeville, was retained to
defend him, and that firm also took up the cases of the rest
as they were brought in. Anticipating trouble, Justice Wall
Hatfield had engaged the services of lawyer Perry Cline,
long before Jeff McCoy was killed, and Cline felt bound in
honor to stand by Wall, even after Jeff was killed. So those
now in prison have the best mountain talent to defend
them.

Writs of habeas corpus, and applications for bail in be-
wildering number and order have been secured and made,
and out of it all Wall Hatfield and Doc Mayhorn find
themselves still in Pikeville jail without hope of release
before trial for the murder of the three McCoy boys. Plyant and Sam Mayhorn are in jail, because unable to raise
$3,000 bail, and the rest have either obtained bail or turned
State's evidence. They will all be tried next February. Dan
Whit voluntarily came over to Kentucky as a witness for
the State.

One feature of the legal proceedings was an appeal to

the national courts by Governor Wilson, of West Virginia, for the release of the Hatfields on the ground that the Constitution provides that no man may be deprived of life or liberty without due process of law. Kidnapping was not due process, but the United States Supreme Court decided that nevertheless the prisoners were lawfully in the custody of the Pike County authorities. Gov. Wilson himself appeared in court as a Hatfield attorney.

Of course, indictments were found in Logan against the Pike County boys for the murder of Uncle Jim Vance and Bill Dempsey, and also for kidnapping the prisoners mentioned. The State of West Virginia offered $100 reward each for the arrest of the Kentucky kidnappers, and $500 for Frank Phillips. The Hatfields offered $500 additional for Phillips. The rewards offered so far for the Hatfield gang are: $1,250 for Cap, $700 for Bad Anse, $700 for Jonce, $500 for Elias, and $100 each for the rest of the indicted men. But Gov. Buckner has promised to offer $500 each for the men engaged in burning the house of old Rand'l'.

One of this house-burning gang has been arrested, and is now in jail at Ironton, Ohio. It is Gillespie. He has made a full and voluntary confession, and as he is but seventeen years old, he will be accepted as a witness by Pike County's attorney, C. Lee Ferguson. His arrest was brought about through the evil passions of Bad Anse. Anse took a fancy to the boy's mother, and straightway drove both boy and father out of the county. The boy was then located by detectives and arrested.

Meantime these Kentuckians were arrested: Dave Stratton, John Norman, John B. Datson, and Joseph Franklin Smith. They are charged with kidnapping and murder, and, as already stated, are here under heavy guard for trial today. They will be defended by McComas & Kelly, Smith & Stratton, and Major Stratton, who is the father of Dave, the defendant.

It would take too much space to relate here all the adventures of the detectives who have made these arrests, but the net they have woven about Frank Phillips is especially interesting. When Jonce Hatfield fled to Colorado, his wife Nancy, a fine-looking mountain girl and a full cousin to the McCoy boys, was asked to assist in arresting Frank Phillips. She readily consented, and to that end went to her mother's house over on Peter Creek, in Pike County. Here she made love to Phillips successfully, and is now his mistress. Phillips stays with her most of his time, living in the one-room cabin with her old mother.

She sends a letter once a week to Superintendent Alf Burnett of the Charleston (West Virginia) detectives, telling him, of Phillips's doings, and the movements of other indicted Kentuckians for whom Burnett's men are looking. She is one of the few mountain women who can write.

Phillips learned of the letter-writing on last Thursday, but whether he has killed the woman, taken to the woods, or refused to believe the report has not been learned. Nancy's method of procedure has the full approval of the Hatfields, who speak of her in the most kindly manner.

Bad Anse, in conversation last Tuesday, said: "Ef I could just shoot that —— Phillips and Ole Rand'l', I'd go to the gallows jest as peert as ever I went to dinner."

His words point the only way to the ending of the war. It has been prolonged only because Gov. Wilson first refused to allow his murderers to be tried, and because Gov. Buckner will not set a good example by returning good for evil in allowing Phillips to be arrested lawfully.

LIST OF MURDERS DURING THE FEUD

Bill Stayton, shot in the back by Sam McCoy, nephew of old Randolph McCoy.

Deacon Ellison Hatfield, shot in the back by Fanner McCoy.

Talbot and Farmer McCoy and Randolph McCoy, Jr., tied to bushes and shot by the Hatfield gang.

Jeff McCoy shot in the back by Cap Hatfield.

Allaphare McCoy shot by Ellison Mounts as she pleaded for life.

Calvin McCoy shot in the back by the Hatfield gang.

Jim Vance, shot through the forehead by Frank Phillips.

Bill Dempsey, shot to death after being wounded and while praying that he might die in peace.

To these should be added the wife of Talbot McCoy, who grieved herself to death over the terrible murder of her husband.

LIST OF THOSE WOUNDED DURING THE FEUD

Hense Scott, shot through the left shoulder, and John Scott, shot through the right knee by the Hatfield gang, who mistook them for McCoys. They are crippled for life.

Mrs. Bill Daniels, ribs broken by Cap Hatfield. Injured for life.

Mrs. Randolph McCoy, two ribs broken by a blow of a gunstock, and head cut open when her home was burned. She will never fully recover.

Tom Mitchell, fingers of left hand shot off by Randolph McCoy.

Jonce Hatfield, shot in the right shoulder by Randolph McCoy with birdshot. Not crippled.

Ellison Mounts, left forearm split with rifle ball by Calvin McCoy. Not crippled.

Budd McCoy, shot through the right shoulder by Hatfield gang when Dempsey was killed. Not crippled.

Cap Hatfield, shot across palm of right hand by Calvin McCoy. Not crippled.

Detective John Knapper, of Charleston, West Virginia, shot through hollow of right foot. Slight wound.

It is said that several other slight wounds have been inflicted on both sides, but no account was taken of them.

The traveler to the abandoned home of old Bad Anse on Tug River, opposite the mouth of Peter Creek, will find over the fireplace a gaudy lithograph motto, which reads:

THERE IS NO PLACE LIKE OUR HOME.

Some one familiar with the history of the locality has scribbled with a lead pencil under the many colored letters this comment:

"Leastwise, not this side of hell."

Forgiveness strengthens the spirit, sweetens temper, stifles anger, extinguishes envy, subdues pride; she bridles the tongue, restrains the hand, tramples upon temptations.

ABOUT THE AUTHOR

John R. Spears (1850-1936) was an author and journalist whose other works include *Master Mariners, The Story of the New England Whalers,* and *The History of Our Navy from Its Origin to the Present Day.*